. . . and walls.

We use paint to spray cars, trucks

. . . and bicycles.

Sometimes we need paint for making signs

. . . **and lines on the ground.**

You can use paint to do lovely pictures or patterns

. . . or for making amazing blob paintings.

You can blow paint, or spray it

. . . or make pictures with your fingers and hands.

powder paint
to mix with water

bottles of paint

water-colour paints

There are all kinds of paint.

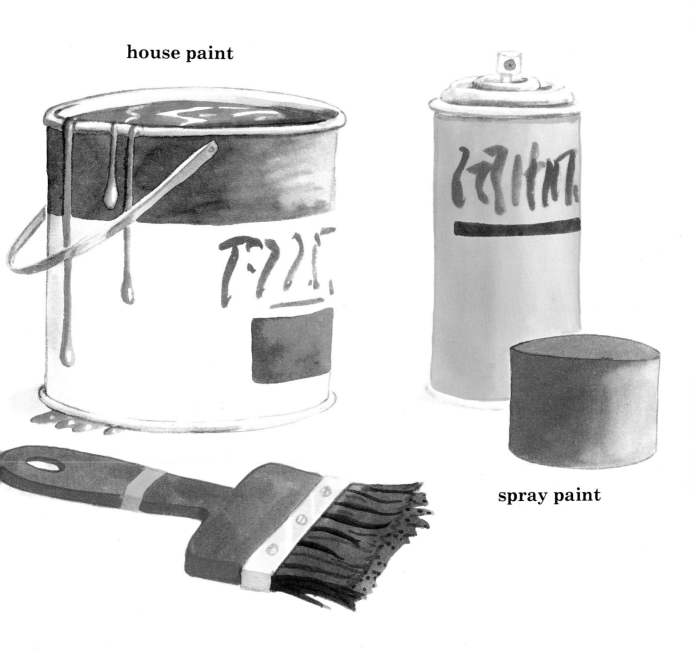

house paint

spray paint

It is used for lots of different things.

Look at the picture.
How many things have been painted red?
How many are yellow, green or blue?